SURVIVE TO THRIVE

NOAH DIDN'T WAIT FOR HIS SHIP TO COME IN...

HE BUILT HIS!

SURVIVE TO THRIVE

NOAH DIDN'T WAIT FOR HIS SHIP TO COME IN...

HE BUILT HIS!

~How to Thrive After a Major Crisis~

FZM Publishing
Copyright 2007
Revised Edition 2017
By Fogzone Ministries
P.O. Box 3707
Hickory, NC. 28603

All Scriptures, unless indicated, are taken from the King James Version

Scripture quotations marked NJKV are taken from the New King James Version

Scripture quotations marked NIV are taken from the New International Version.

ISBN

978-0-9977689-3-0

Printed in the United States of America.

Foreword

For the world, these are the worst of days. The intensity of social unrest that surrounds the globe is unprecedented, as entire nations selfishly think nothing of selling their proverbial souls for a bigger piece of the global financial pie.

Furthermore, life seems to be going by faster than any man can catch it. Throughout the ages there have been those who are the peddlers and panhandlers of hope. These men and women who desire to become your cheerleaders when times are only disturbed by winds of our own choices that blow in the storms of consequences deserved.

In the midst of all this turmoil, there is an unprecedented time quickly coming upon us. These are the days that men and women from the four corners of the earth, like never before, will unite under the banner of Divine Faith. Their Faith will be contrary to the popular religious rhetoric that has been handed to us from past generations.

These chosen ones will begin to gather and recognize that there is a Goliath in the world that must be dealt with, and a world full of sin that must be resisted. They will recognize that there is a commitment to God that demands a holiness to ever really see Him beyond the Floods of Life that must be out lasted.

In order to understand the signs of the times, we must look to those in history; those that will choose, like Moses, to suffer with the people of God rather than enjoy the pleasures of sin for a season. In the life of Noah, we see one of the greatest examples of a man rising from the ash heaps of life to touch Heaven. His resolve led to the salvation of mankind, as we know it.

On the pages of this timely book, you will see a step-by-step process to help you turn your mourning into dancing... your gloom into joy... and defeat into victory. *Dr. Grillo*, a man who was brought from a place of loss to victory to loss and onto victory again, is fully equipped to teach us on this subject... *Embrace these truths and discover your destiny...*

Dr. Robert Daniels Thompson
Senior Pastor of Family Harvest Church
And founder of the Winning in Life Ministries

PREFACE

No matter how good we are, everyone will have to live through some form of conflict, droughts, and crisis. Pain and crisis are a part of our everyday life, which includes calamities, relational hurts, a wandering child, some natural disaster or even racial slander. If you do not know or understand your eternal purpose, you will become disappointed and depressed to the point of giving up in the midst of a crisis.

I was sitting in my office thinking about all the terrible tragedies we've been witnessing in the news lately. As I sat searching for answers, the Lord revealed to me that our present generation has not seen a crisis like the one that took place during the days of Noah.

No one has seen a storm like the storm of that day; a storm so fierce and devastating that it took God only forty days to cover the entire earth with water. Even the tsunamis and hurricanes that have laid our lands in total chaos and pain can't compare to the crisis that Noah and his entire family had to live through.

If Noah could survive and thrive after the worst of the worse storms ever recorded, then why can't we? I have taken the time to extract information from Noah's life to help us also SURVIVE TO THRIVE AGAIN!

Dr. Jerry A. Grillo, Jr.

INTRODUCTION

Many people in this world sit around waiting for God, or someone like God, to enter their existence and rescue them from their life of failure and mistakes.

I've often left people's atmosphere feeling frustrated and annoyed after listening to them speak about walking in faith, and trusting God for a supernatural miracle despite their terrible decisions. Granted, these people are attempting to improve their life, but let me encourage all who fit this category; mistakes always bring about consequences. Pay them, and get on with it!

Those who sit on their hind end day after day, confessing that they are going to be wealthy set me ablaze; I just want to scream, "Stop confessing wealth and health if you are not willing to do something about it!"

Noah didn't sit around waiting for his ship to come in...Noah built his!

My hope is that this book will supply you with the proper motivation to believe in yourself enough to go after your dreams. If you have no dream, get one! If you have no desires, cultivate some! If you have no goals, set them! If you need money, work for it! If you need wealth, build it! I'm not writing this book, sitting on a heap of money, reaching down to the "little pipsqueak" so that I can sell another get-rich-quick scheme.

The purpose of this book is to motivate you to believe in yourself. That's all. God has anointed me to be a motivator. God has called me to reach down and help others succeed, to pull them out of holes. What kind of holes, you may ask? Any holes- from drugs to relationships! Many have found themselves in the hole of life, seeing only dirt walls of defeat, disgust, discouragement, and depression. Until you believe that God wants you wealthy, you will never pursue any form of His blessings.

Read and learn, at least what I know. I believe that this book will help you reach for the *real* you. You are God's handiwork; don't you think it's time to act like it?

NOAH CREATED A CLIMATE OF SUCCESS AND SURVIVAL

The greatest catastrophe ever recorded in history was the storm that occurred in Noah's day. There has not been a storm since then that has had the same effect with the same potential. This storm wiped out the whole world, with the exception of Noah and his entire family.

Noah survived to thrive again; so can you, and so can I!

TABLE OF CONTENT

Foreword	v
Preface	vii
Introduction	ix
Noah Found Favor	13
Noah Protected Himself	19
Labor to Hear God's Voice	25
Noah Followed an Instruction	31
Success will Require Faith	41
Noah was a Family Man	49
Noah was a Worshipper	59
Noah Worked Through Criticism	67
Noah was a Seed Sower	73
Noah Possessed Patience	83
Noah Succeeded in Spite of Opposition	91
Reactions Decide Action	99
Conclusion	113

CHAPTER ONE

NOAH FOUND FAVOR IN THE EYES OF THE LORD

SEEK THE FAVOR OF GOD, NOT THE FAVOR OF MEN!

Many have succeeded in life; many have survived the raging storm, because they were simply favored by God. Although this book isn't exclusively centered on favor, its main theme urges us to walk in favor.

People of Noah's days didn't walk in righteousness. Most of the people of Noah's time were fulfilling their own lusts and desires, and God had not shown His hand of power since the Garden of Eden. Men are ruled only by their own natural powers to be satisfied; we will stray from what is right without the restraint of laws and parameters.

> *"The LORD saw how great the wickedness of the human race had become on the earth, and that every inclination of the thoughts of the human heart was only evil all the time. The LORD regretted that he had made human beings on the earth, and his heart was deeply troubled. So the LORD said, "I will wipe from the face of the earth the human race I have created—and with them the animals, the birds and the creatures that move along the ground—for I regret that I have made them." Genesis 6:5-7 NIV*

What caused such wickedness? Man's thoughts are evil. We don't need a devil to ruin our lives. All God has to do is turn us over to ourselves... no devil in hell can hurt us as bad as we can hurt ourselves.

God was so angry with mankind that He decided to wipe it out. But wait! One man found favor in the eyes of the Lord.

"But Noah found favor in the eyes of the LORD." Genesis 6:8 NIV

No one will ever succeed and thrive to be a success without walking in favor. Favor is simply someone liking you enough to help you exit the season you are in; someone who is in the season that you desire to be in, and who is willing to

FAVOR WILL SCHEDULE UNCOMMON SEASONS BUT FAITH DECIDES FAVOR'S TIMING

enter your season to mentor you out. I've written several books on favor and can say that no one, including Noah, can survive life without favor. Favor isn't some new theology that we have created for the twenty-first century church so that we can write books and build our ministries. No Sir!

In the book of Zechariah we read a verse that most Christians know: ***"Not by might, not by power, but by my spirit says the Lord"*** (Paraphrased Zechariah 4:6).

This passage is referring to the insurmountable task that Zerubbabel had to face when he was about to take on the job of rebuilding the ruined temple.

You have to understand that the temple was left destroyed, and there wasn't one stone left on top of another. He faced what seemed to be an impossible task. Most of God's instructions are irrational, but they are never impossible. Every person who has succeeded for God had to do it facing danger, toil, and snares. They had to possess a strong sense of courage and obedience.

That's where favor belongs... to those who are willing to risk it all to gain it all!

How about you? Are you one of those rare jewels sitting in the dark crevasses of life, waiting for your moment to be discovered; hoping that someone or something will come along to remove the dirt that's been hiding your value and worth; someone who has hope that there is more than what others are seeing? Hidden in the vast illusion of your image is the real you waiting to fulfill its purpose.

Those who are willing to follow the instructions, even if they seem to be strange and irrational, attract the favor of God and man. Noah was one of those rare jewels...Abraham was one of those rare jewels... so was Zerubbabel.

> *"So he answered and said to me: This is the word of the LORD to Zerubbabel, Not by might or by power, but by My Spirit, says the LORD of hosts." Who are you, O Great Mountain? Before Zerubbabel you shall become a plain! And he shall bring forth the capstone with shouts of **"Grace, grace to it**!" Zechariah 4:6-7 NKJV*

Notice the last words "Grace, Grace." Remember grace means favor... Favor, Favor! He had to speak favor to the capstone every day. The capstone represented the last stone that was to be placed on the finished product. Zerubbabel had to speak favor (grace) to his future in order to exit his present. He had to visualize where he was supposed to be, not where he was. Speak into the season you desire to be in, rather than the one you are in.

I believe we are living in a time where the purpose of grace is being abused. The power of grace is being cheapened. I believe it's called "hyper grace" Grace is not God showing pity on your situation, and it is not a permission to slip to live out fleshly desires. Grace is God's empowerment to overcome the errors of your life and accomplish the plan of God.

Noah was given favor. Noah was empowered by God to fulfill his destiny. Noah found favor in the eyes of the Lord and so can YOU!

KEYS ON HOW TO EXIT YOUR PRESENT SEASON:

1. *Until you despise your present, your future will never materialize.*
2. *Stop focusing on your past and start reaching toward your future.*
3. *Start thinking and talking like you are already in your future.*
4. *Have faith in your destiny.*
5. *Honor those who are in the season you desire to be in.*
6. *Celebrate your difference.*
7. *Pursue the information you need to enter your next season.*

CHAPTER TWO

NOAH PROTECTED HIMSELF FROM THE ACTIONS OF THE UNGODLY...

"And God looked upon the earth, and, behold, it was corrupt; for all flesh had corrupted his way upon the earth."
Genesis 6:12

You may not qualify in man's eyes, but you qualify in God's eyes. Noah didn't fit into modern society. He excluded himself from the majority to protect himself and his family from the sins of the world. No one will ever succeed without the power of God's favor. Everybody needs to activate the favor of God. But God's favor is connected to the family. Protect your family at all cost.

What you let around you will determine what comes out of you.

To succeed and find God's best in your life, you must adopt a qualification process by which you evaluate those you let into your atmosphere.

ATMOSHERE MATTERS! It's obvious that Noah was looked upon as being weird and abnormal. Noah **didn't fit in**! He wouldn't do what everybody else was doing. As I said earlier, you may not qualify in man's eyes, but you qualify in God's eyes. The only person you have to please in your life is God.

I have found that when you begin to build your belief system and live by it, those around you will begin to persecute you for it. My son and I were talking one day about how easy it is to fall in the trap of acting, talking, and thinking like the world. My son has a very good mind for his age, and so I began to teach him that the reason it seems so easy for him to follow the world is that he lacks his own convictions of what is right and wrong. I explained to him that as long as he lives according to my persuasions he will always have questions, but as he develops his own standards, his own beliefs, his own personal convictions, he will become more equipped to fight the mainstream to be different. This is true for everyone. *You are only celebrated for your difference...*

YOUR PROBLEM MAY NOT BE WHAT'S IN YOUR LIFE BUT WHO IS IN YOUR LIFE

Your problems in life are usually the result of those whom you have chosen to listen to or hang out with.

PEOPLE YOU NEED TO AVOID; they are dangerous to your success.

1. *Those who feed your doubts.*
2. *Those who trivialize your passion.*
3. *Those who feed your weaknesses.*
4. *Those who ease your pain in a bad decision.*
5. *Those who are comfortable in the presence of the ungodly.*
6. *Those who are comfortable in the presence of your enemies.*
7. *Those who call themselves your friend but will not defend you in your absence.*
8. *Those who never feed your faith.*
9. *Those who become jealous of your success or promotions.*

It's not what's on your ship, but who is on your ship that is costing you...

Jonah decided to board a ship to flee from God's instruction to go to Nineveh. A storm began to gather around the ship on its destination. The clouds grew fierce, the rains crashed down, the wind began to pick up waves, and the vessel began to sink. The men tried to paddle the ship back to safety with all their might, but to no avail. They had no idea what to do so they began to throw off all their supplies and resources, and they depleted themselves of all their possessions.

Notice how the wrong person connected to you can cost you greatly; you may have to survive a storm that was scheduled for someone else. Not everyone around you belongs around you. It's time to start qualifying those hanging around, and not just around you but also around your children.

Wrong connections can be very costly.

After the people realized that their efforts to survive the storm weren't working, Jonah, who was hiding in the ship, came forward and confessed that the problem wasn't caused by *what* was on the ship, but by *who* was on the ship. So, when they threw Jonah from the ship, the storm immediately ceased...

> "So they picked up Jonah and threw him into
> the sea, and the sea ceased from its raging."
> Jonah 1:15 NKJV

IT'S NOT WHAT'S ON YOUR SHIP BUT WHO! *Not everyone around you belongs around you...*

Wrong people can cause wrong things to happen. Guard your life. A Godly life is not a protected life; a godly life is a vulnerable life. You have to decide how you are going to protect your life. Remember, what's hanging around you will determine what is coming out of you. Your future is decided by whose voice you have chosen to believe.

Let me give you the formula for advancement.

1. **Awareness**: The ability to know or realize what needs to stay or what needs to be sent away. You can't fix what you are unable to see. You must become aware of what's happening in your environment. This is important. If you do not assess the environment you could be giving your enemy valuable information.
2. **Understanding:** The mental quality and power to think and know. To have specific interpretation. This is a powerful tool. The ability to understand. No one will ever advance without understanding. Wisdom is powerless without understanding. Financial lack is a clue you lack understanding. Relational breakdowns are a clue you lack understanding. Wisdom is to know how; understanding is to know why. Pray for understanding.
3. **Disassociation:** The ability to walk away. Never stay where you are not welcome. Never stay where you are not celebrated. Bad company corrupts good morals, attitudes, and decisions. God would not bless Abraham fully until He

walked away from Lot, his cousin. But when Lot was removed, God blessed Abraham from all four corners of the earth.

4. **Declaration:** The ability to talk about where you are going and not where you came from. The Bible says that if we declare a thing it will be established. Stop talking about what you've been through and start talking about where you are going. Begin to declare your greatness. Begin to speak to your future. Stop all negative talk immediately.

CHAPTER THREE

LABOR TO HEAR THE VOICE OF GOD

"And God said unto Noah..." Genesis 6:13

NOAH KNEW GOD'S VOICE...

I should say, *"Noah labored to **listen** to God's voice"* instead of *"labored to **hear**."* Just because I *hear* the noises that are in a room doesn't necessarily mean that I am *listening* to those noises. Many times people have talked to me, and although I heard what they were saying, I didn't listen because my mind was focused on other things. I was *hearing* but not *listening*. Jesus said that people can hear, yet never understand.

"IT IS THE PROVINCE OF KNOWLEDGE TO SPEAK, AND IT IS THE PRIVILEGE OF WISDOM TO LISTEN." OLIVER WENDELL HOLMES

"...You will be ever hearing but never understanding; you will be ever seeing but never perceiving." Matthew 13:14 NIV

To walk in understanding, you have to do more than just hear; you have to *listen* to what is being said.

"Nevertheless, listen to what I have to say in your hearing and in the hearing of all the people." Jeremiah 28:7 NIV

There is a big difference between hearing and listening. *Hearing* is the act or process of perceiving sounds. *Listening* is making a conscious effort to hear, to attend closely to what is being said. It simply means to "pay close attention" and to "take advice."

The men of Noah's time were wicked and did not even have the desire to hear, much less the ear to hear anything from a holy and righteous God. It's obvious that Noah had a spiritual ear to hear, and not just to hear but also to *recognize* the voice of God. He had to be a man of principle; a man that kept his standards higher than the society that was speaking and living around him.

Favor Key: *What you keep hearing you will eventually believe.*

You must understand that whomever you allow to speak to you is forging what you are becoming. What you choose to listen to you will eventually believe. What you believe you will eventually do and become.

WATCH OUT FOR THE SECOND VOICE...

If someone changes their opinion of you, it is usually due to a second voice they have chosen to listen to. The power of this truth is clear. God had a garden (Eden) where everything was perfect, at least until another voice was heard speaking in that garden; a voice that questioned the instructions that were given in that garden; a voice that merged deception with true statements. It's not that the other voice in and of itself had the power to deceive; rather the other voice gained power because there was an ear given to it.

I believe that Adam and Eve were already defeated when they chose to *listen*. That other voice has a very strong and powerful attraction; once one gives attention to it; one finds it almost impossible not to be persuaded. If this voice (whomever it may be) is not speaking what God has already said, then it is speaking to do harm and not good.

The other voice destroyed the perfect harmony of the one true voice. The same is true for our churches, homes, schools, and relationships. If we give that other voice an ear, we will destroy the harmony of what is good and perfect. We must qualify whom we allow to speak to us, or better yet, whom we choose to listen to.

Let's spend some time on this; it will help us to survive a lot of church and relationship chaos.

> *"Now the serpent was more crafty (cunning) than any of the wild animals the LORD God had made. He said to the woman, "Did God really say, 'You must not eat from any tree in the garden'?" Genesis 3:1 NIV*

The word that gets me here is, *"crafty"* or *"cunning,"* the King James Version uses the word *"subtle."*

Webster's Dictionary defines *"cunning"* as getting what is wanted in a clever and often deceptive way; cleverness or skill especially at tricking people in order to get something.[i]

Never think for one moment that this other voice is stupid or lacks the wisdom to deceive. Our biggest mistake when fighting the enemy is assuming that he's weak. Evil is alive and well!

Labor to hear the true voice; it is the only voice that will set you free. You can identify someone's voice only after listening to it for days and years. Many of us say that, "God has said," and the truth is that God didn't say a word. *Spirits have voices; Feelings have voices; Attitudes have voices; People have voices; Addictions have voices.* No wonder people live in a sea of mass confusion and paranoia. It is a wonder that we can stay focused enough to finish this manuscript with so many voices in our heads. We must labor to hear the only voice that will set us free – God's voice.

CHAPTER FOUR

NOAH FOLLOWED AN IRRATIONAL INSTRUCTION

"And God said unto Noah... Thus did Noah; according to all that God commanded him, so did he." Genesis 6:13, 22

The difference between seasons is an instruction. When God was ready to change Noah's season, He gave him an instruction; "NOAH, BUILD AN ARK!" God instructed Noah to build an ark that would allow him to move from a place of defeat to a place of purity and holiness.

GOD WILL NEVER MOVE YOU PAST YOUR LAST ACT OF DISOBEDIENCE
DR. MIKE MURDOCK

When God was ready to change Moses' season from tending his father-in-law's sheep to becoming one of history's greatest leaders, He gave him an instruction. "Moses, tell Pharaoh to let my people go!"

There is a great story in Second Kings, chapter five about a man whose name was Naaman.

> *"Now Naaman, captain of the host of the king of Syria, was a great man with his master, and honourable, because by him the LORD had given deliverance unto Syria: he was also a mighty man in valour, but he was a leper." 2 Kings 5:1 KJV*

Naaman was a great man; he was a mighty and strong leader. The Word of God calls him a man of honor, a man whom the Lord used to defeat an enemy. He is also called a mighty man of valor. He was a good man, but Naaman had a problem... *"He was a leper."*
Good people have to weather bad seasons sometimes.

Crisis isn't always a sign that you are living wrong, or doing wrong things. Bad things happen to good people.

Now, I could digress and preach this phrase until everybody in the house is in an uproar. No matter how much we do, no matter how great we are, trouble can still find us! The King of Israel sent Naaman to see one of God's greatest prophets – the prophet Elisha.

> *"So Naaman went with his horses and chariots and stopped at the door of Elisha's house. Elisha sent a messenger to say to him,* **"Go, wash yourself seven times in the Jordan, and your flesh will be restored and you will be cleansed."** *2 Kings 5:9-10 NIV*

Notice that the prophet didn't require Naaman to sow. He didn't ask him to pray and fast for days; all Elisha required of Naaman was to follow a simple instruction. "Go and wash yourself seven times in the Jordan River and you will be made clean."

The prophet didn't heal him; Naaman wasn't healed because of charity, or by sowing, not even by prayer, or fasting. He was healed because he was willing to follow the instruction.

This does not dismiss God as the chief end of all. We understand that God is the result of the miracle. God is the healer and the deliver.

What healed Naaman? What cured His leprosy? No one

laid a hand on him. No one anointed him with oil. He wasn't at church worshipping until God's healing power fell upon him! He wasn't in a healing crusade, and yet Naaman did receive his miracle.

But Naaman was not pleased with the way the prophet dealt with him. You may not the like the message, but don't hate the messenger. Actually, Naaman was quite offended at how he was treated.

> *"But Naaman went away angry and said, "I thought that he would surely come out to me and stand and call on the name of the LORD his God, wave his hand over the spot and cure me of my leprosy." 2 Kings 5:11 NIV*

Naaman felt disgraced; he should have been important enough for the man of God to come out and at least shake his hand. Instead, Elisha just sent him an instruction.

DON'T PLACE PRE-CONCEIVED IDEAS ON HOW GOD IS GOING TO BLESS YOU... LEAVE IT UP TO GOD!

Would you rather have a visit from a prophet, or an instruction that will produce your miracle?

Naaman was healed because he followed an instruction; a miracle is scheduled at the end of each act of obedience. Let me ask you something; *could you be missing a miracle today simply because you have refused to follow a Godly instruction?* God views disobedience with distained eyes. He is more impressed with our willingness to obey Him than with our sacrifices of praise and offerings.

> "...Does the LORD delight in burnt offerings and sacrifices as much as in obeying the voice of the LORD? To obey is better than sacrifice, and to heed is better than the fat of rams. For rebellion is like the sin of divination, and arrogance like the evil of idolatry..." 1 Samuel 15:22-23 NIV

FACTS ABOUT DISOBEDIENCE:

- *Disobedience can delay your scheduled miracle.*
- *Disobedience can demoralize your future.*
- *God will never take you past your last act of disobedience.*
- *Disobedience can hinder a move of God in your life.*
- *Disobedience can destroy what God has already blessed.*
- *Disobedience is proof that you haven't surrendered to the will of God.*
- *Disobedience is proof that you don't trust God.*

FACTS ABOUT INSTRUCTIONS:

- *Every instruction carries within it a key to the door of your next season.*
- *The instructions you're willing to follow can propel you into your future.*

- *The difference between where you are and where you would like to be is an instruction.*
- *An ignored instruction is costly and possibly deadly.*
- *Until you follow the first instruction you will never walk into the next one.*

Noah and his entire family were saved from the terrible storm because Noah followed an ***irrational instruction***. He was willing to risk it all for the sake of obedience. Instead of losing it all, he actually received it all. God encoded the power to live in the instruction. Noah and his family would have ended up like everyone else if he had not followed the instruction.

MIRACLES ARE SCHEDULED TO THOSE WHO FOLLOW THE INSTRUCTIONS!

Do what Noah did! Follow Godly instruction. I promise you will find that the Lord has already scheduled your miracle.

Miracles are placed at the end of every instruction. ***An instruction may appear to be irrational but it is not impossible.*** Remember, when God gives an instruction He will require faith to carry it out. God will rarely give you an instruction that is within your natural reach. He will usually give you an instruction that will *strain* and *stretch you* out of your normal self. Attached to this instruction is the power of believing God for a miracle. The supernatural is tied to an instruction.

- *"Moses, stretch out your hand and pick up the rod..."*
- *"Moses, go and tell Pharaoh to let my people go..."*

- *"Joshua, go and defeat Jericho..."*
- *"Naaman, dip seven times in the Jordan..."*

There is another story in the Bible that has always fascinated me. It is found in the book of Luke, chapter six. It was the Sabbath, the crowd was present and the leadership was ready to accuse Jesus for being disobedient for doing well on the Sabbath. There was a man in the crowd with a **withered hand.**

YOU CAN HAVE WHAT NOAH HAD... IF YOU DO WHAT NOAH DID!

> *"On another Sabbath he went into the synagogue and was teaching, and a man was there whose right hand was shriveled. The Pharisees and the teachers of the law were looking for a reason to accuse Jesus, so they watched him closely to see if he would heal on the Sabbath." Luke 6:6-7 NIV*

This is religion at its best...leaders who see the need, but wait for someone else to take care of it! Then respond in jealously and wrath when someone else finally does. Churches are full of such people. They always look to see who is going to be blessed or touched, but have anger and jealousy as the meal for the day when such a blessing occurs.

There are two kinds of people in each crowd; both will notice the need, but only one is there for the benefit of change.

I love Jesus in this passage. Jesus knew that the leaders were determined to catch Him at something to discredit Him. He knew that they had also noticed the man with the withered hand. He knew that they were watching Him to see if He would respond to this man's need; if He'd do something about it. Jesus didn't disappoint them.

Jesus called this man out in front of everyone and asked him to pull his ugly, withered hand from hiding – to stretch it forth! *Once again there is an instruction given for a miracle to emerge.*

Now, place yourself in this story. Imagine what must have been going through this person's mind, much less the crowd's and the Pharisees' minds.

I bet the religious leaders were thinking, *"Man, this couldn't get any better. Jesus is not just going to heal this man; He's going to do in it front of everybody. Jesus is going to break a Sabbath law to heal a man with a withered hand!*

Now, think about the man with the withered hand. I can imagine how embarrassed this man must have been. After all, he's been accustomed to keeping that ugly, useless limb in hiding. I wonder how many times in his life he had to endure someone looking and snickering, or pointing and laughing at that gross hand attached to his body?

I believe this hand exemplifies those things in our lives

that have become withered by time, loss, and pain; *withered visions, hopes, dreams, relationships, finances, etc.* We have become this man in our own lives. We have been hiding and covering what has become withered, shriveled up, dried up, and emaciated. What was once alive is now dead. Can you relate? Jesus assessed the crowd and noticed the man with the withered hand.

What have you been hiding? Do you want to be healed of it? If so, you're going to have to be willing to do what this man did. You're going to have to bring it out of hiding. You're going to have to stretch in faith to give it to Jesus. Somewhere in the middle of that stretching, your life will be made clean, whole, and healed.

> *"And when He had looked around at them all, He said to the man, "Stretch out your hand." And he did so, and his hand was restored as whole as the other." Luke 6:10 NKJV*

God has designed a certain pattern for us to walk in, so that He can deliver us from our mess. God will hide your sin and help you overcome it when you freely expose your weakness in His presence, but God will allow the enemy to expose you when you choose to hide your sin. The secret to *overcoming* is to confess your problems daily to God and stop hiding what He already knows. Go ahead! Stretch out that withered hand. God is about to do something supernatural with it. Follow the instructions to the letter.

If God was willing to do what He did for Noah, He will do the same for you. Do you want what Noah had? Do what Noah did!

CHAPTER FIVE

SUCCESS WILL REQUIRE INCREDIBLE FAITH AND TRUST IN GOD

NOAH BUILT A SHIP WITHOUT A RUDDER...

Noah possessed incredible faith and trust in god

The Bible tells us that it is impossible to please God without faith (Hebrews 11:6). Faith is the one currency every believer needs to build. You can do nothing in the realm of the Spirit void of faith.

- *You're saved by faith.*
- *You're healed by faith* (Matt. 9:22).
- *You're delivered by faith.*
- *You're set free by faith.*
- *You're made righteous by faith.*

Noah possessed incredible faith; he built a ship without a rudder. A rudder is the instrument used to guide the direction of a ship. When Noah entered into the Ark with his family, he entered into a trust that few have ever experienced. He had no control over where he was going. When Noah entered the Ark, he placed his life and his family's lives into the hands of God. Noah's action conveyed that we are to trust God no matter what our journey may entail.

FAITH IS BUILDING A SHIP WITHOUT A RUDDER!

What incredible faith; to trust no matter what! Think for a moment what total abandonment it is to board a ship, not knowing its destination, and to have no future resources except one – God! That's faith. We must trust God with our destination if we are traveling on a ship without a rudder. The Bible says that *a righteous person's steps are ordered by the Lord* (Psalms 37:23).

Imagine for a moment what it must have felt like to hear the voice of God at such a time when His voice wasn't fluent. But when God finally spoke, He gave Noah the instruction to build a ship. God gave Noah the exact blueprint for the ship and the reason it must be built – it was going to rain! It had never rained prior to that moment. Nevertheless, Noah was asked to build a vessel and to believe in something that he had never experienced. Not only was it going to rain, it was going to rain enough to cover the whole earth. For Noah to survive, he had to build an ARK! Build it with ***one door and one window***.

Here's the catch; Noah was given power over the window but not the door. When God shut the door, Noah was no longer able to open it. So when Noah and his family entered the ARK, they were to remain there until God opened the door. They did not know how long that would be.

This required more faith than I've ever seen. Only God had the power over the door. The ARK was a type of Christ. The Ark represented the power of being in Christ. Once you've entered in, you must trust God for your journey. God didn't leave Noah blind. He placed a window in the ARK to give Noah a look into his next season.

The door represents the passageway to a new season or dimension. The window gives you the power to see into that next season or dimension. If you were placed into a room with four walls but no door, you would be confined to that room for life. If you were to be in that same room with only a window big enough to see out, you'd be able to look at another place, but you would not be able to get there. Windows give us the power to see. A door gives us the power to move through it and toward what we see. I've often heard that faith is not seeing but believing. I tend to disagree! Faith is seeing. To move from one dimension to another will require sight, not human sight, not human understanding, but faith built on God's sight. We must see it God's way.

Noah had an *Epiphany*. An *Epiphany* is what has always been there but has just now been revealed. What has always been apparent to God is now apparent to you! You now begin to see what God sees. The following story in Second Kings, chapter six gives the best example of what I'm talking about.

Elisha was surrounded by the enemy. When Elisha's servant opened the tent and saw the enemy encamped around them, he tried to inform Elisha who didn't even act concerned. He informed the prophet again, "Elisha, we are outnumbered and the enemy has found us out – it's over!"

Elisha grabbed his servant and prayed, "God open my servant's eyes, so that he can see." Then he told him to open the tent and to *take another look*. When his servant did, he exclaimed in amazement that he could now see a swarm of allies...the army of God was encamped around the enemy.

Now, here's where it gets interesting. What really happened? It's obvious that the Lord's army was always there. We further know that the servant wasn't blind, even though the prophet asked God to open his servant's eyes that he might see. I'll tell you what happened. God opened the window! Before you go through any door, you should first look out of the window. Elisha and his servant escaped untouched. As a matter of fact, they walked right through the middle of their enemy. God had blinded the enemy, or perhaps hid the two servants in another dimension.

Noah had to see. He had to see what God was seeing. When Noah looked to see what God was seeing, his faith grew. Noah was able to build a ship without a rudder. He did it in spite of his critics; he did it in spite of what he didn't know; he did it in spite of what others were saying; and he did it in spite of his fears.

Noah operated on what God told him. He moved and worked his **FAITH**! Faith gives you the power to step out on God's Word alone. Faith is the key that unlocks the doorway to your next season. Remember, we have no power over the door, just the window.

- Wisdom determines your favor.
- Favor schedules your seasons.
- Faith decides favor's timing.

Timing is a very important key to increase and change. You can have the right idea but if it is implemented at the wrong time, it becomes the wrong idea in timing.

Time is now; Timing is tomorrow.

We live in time. God exist in timing. We always exist in now; God exist in and outside of time! What I do in time decides what happens in timing. I can never live in timing I can only live in now. What I do now decides what happens next (timing). Timing is a key to accelerated increase. When you exercise timing you are activating your faith in time. Faith is the key to divine timing. I exercise my faith now which gives me the ability to adapt and adjust my life to prepare to experience God's timing for my future. Faith is the ability to wait with expectation long enough for God to adjust, or make suitable in timing, what you have believed for in time.

Faith waits for God to do in time what you desire on time, in the right time, for God's timing.

No one will be able to survive a crisis void of having faith. There must be this sense of hope that no matter how bad it is, or how bad it was, your life is going to turn around for your good and for God's glory.

FACTS ABOUT FAITH

- ***Faith gives you strength to stand...*** *"...If you do not stand firm in your faith, you will not stand at all."*

Isaiah 7:9 NIV

- **Faith produces peace...** *"Open the gates that the righteous nation may enter, the nation that keeps faith. You will keep in perfect peace him whose mind is steadfast, because he trusts in you." Isaiah 26:2-3 NIV*

- **Faith proves you're righteous...** *"...But the righteous person will live by his faithfulness." Habakkuk 2:4 NIV*

- **Broken Faith wearies the heart of God...** *"...So be on your guard and do not be unfaithful. You have wearied the LORD with your words..." Malachi 2:16-17 NIV*

- **Faith produces miracles...** *"And he did not do many miracles there because of their lack of faith." Matthew 13:58 NIV*

- **Small Faith can produce great miracles...** *"...If you have faith as small as a mustard seed, you can say to this mulberry tree, 'Be uprooted and planted in the sea,' and it will obey you." Luke 17:6 NIV*

- **Faith builds a shield around you...** *"Who through faith are shielded by God's power until the coming of the salvation that is ready to be revealed in the last time." 1 Peter 1:5 NIV*

- **Faith is required to stand firm...** *"Resist him, standing firm in the faith, because you know that the family of believers throughout the world are undergoing the same kind of sufferings." 1 Peter 5:9 NIV*

- **Faith provides the power to overcome...** *"For everyone born of God overcomes the world. This is* *the victory that has overcome the world, even our faith." 1 John 5:4 NIV*

- ***Faith tears down the enemies' walls...***
  (Hebrews 11:30)
- ***Faith is the master key to spiritual adoption...***
  (Galatians 5:5)
- ***Faith opens the doors to approach God...***
  (Ephesians 3:12)
- ***Faith is a shield that protects us in times of war...***
  (Ephesians 6:16)
- ***Faith has a voice...*** (Colossians 1:4)

CHAPTER SIX

NOAH PLACED HIS FAMILY AT THE TOP OF HIS PRIORITY LIST!

"The LORD then said to Noah, "Go into the ark, you and your whole family, because I have found you righteous in this generation."
Genesis 7:1 NIV

"You don't really understand human nature unless you know why a child on a merry-go-round will wave at his parents every time around - and why his parents will always wave back." William D. Tammeus[ii]

Don't get so caught up doing the good things in life that you forget the best things. Family is the best thing!

All throughout the Bible, God identifies Himself as the God of Abraham, Isaac, and Jacob.

> *"...I am the God of your father, the God of Abraham, the God of Isaac and the God of Jacob." At this, Moses hid his face, because he was afraid to look at God." Exodus 3:6 NIV*

It is obvious that God is a God of linage; that He wants to be identified as the God of families. With this in mind, it appears that if we don't give up on a family member, God won't either. I believe that since Abraham never gave up on his cousin, Lot, that God never gave up on Lot either.

God would have killed Lot in Sodom *if* Abraham had not spoken to God about him *(Genesis 18)*. Because Abraham interceded for Lot and his family, God sent Angels to get them out to spare them. God is a God of linage, a God of family.

Noah found favor in the eyes of the Lord because he kept his family protected; he kept them away from the wickedness that was so rampant in his day. Noah was a family man. He was a good father, and he was a good husband by providing for his family. He heard from God for his family.

THE FAMILY MATTERS TO GOD

My son plays sports, and I'm the kind of father who rarely misses my children's events. Often, while I am sitting in the stands, my heart grows weary because I notice many more children playing than parents watching. There always seems to be too many kids and too few parents.

For instance, I attended my son's very first wrestling tournament. He was winning every match, and at the end of a long day, he was wrestling for the **GOLD.** I was really impressed.

> **40 PERCENT OF AMERICAN CHILDREN WILL GO TO SLEEP TONIGHT WITHOUT A FATHER PRESENT IN THE HOUSE.**

Due to a mix-up, my son had to wrestle his own teammate, his friend, who had been in the heavy weight division all year. It was quite a match right down to the last second! Both boys were tied with a score of five points, when the opponent scored two points within the very last minute. The game ended with a score of five to seven; my son had lost the game.

My heart sank! My head went down, not because I was ashamed, but because I could see the grief – the disappointment – the pain of defeat on my son's face. Let me tell you, he was disappointed! He walked over to the wall, slid down, put his face in his hands, and cried.

However, the focus of this story is not really my son, but on his friend who won the gold medal. This young boy was a gracious winner. He walked right over to my son to console him; he was more concerned about his friend's loss than his own victory.

My son and I were just leaving the once noisy and crowded gym that now lay silent and empty, when I saw the gold medalist sitting on the bleachers waiting for his bus. I also noticed the deep concern in this boy's eyes as he looked up at me; he was concerned for my son. He asked me to tell Jerry that it was a good match; that it could have gone either way. I told him, "Son, I'm proud of you, you did great." He smiled as I was walking away.

I looked back because something seemed very wrong to me. Here was a gold winner sitting on the bleachers, rubbing and looking at his medal, admiring his accomplishments, and yet this scene seemed out of place and very abnormal. This boy was sitting there all by himself! NO ONE was there to cheer for him. No one cheered for him all day; no mom, no dad, no aunt, no uncle, no one… just a fourteen year old boy sitting all by himself, enjoying his victory.

WHERE WAS HIS FAMILY?

Then it dawned on me. You can see it in the sad eyes of a Cub Scout Leader as he greets only two of all the many dads who were asked to help at their sons' special troop event. You see it in the searching eyes of young boys in the inner city, who look up to gang members as their family.

You see it in the hollow eyes of a single mom as she tries to put her children to bed, as they beg to know where daddy is, while dad has long left with another woman. You see it every single day in the sad eyes of children in schools and on playgrounds; children that have lost their sense of identity because they have no family life.

In his book, *Fatherless American,* David Blankenhorn, founder of the Institute for American Values[iii], writes:

"A generation ago, an American child could reasonably expect to grow up with his or her father. Today, an American child can reasonably expect not to.... This astonishing fact is reflected in many statistics, but here are the two most important: Tonight, about forty percent of American children will go to sleep in homes in which their fathers do not live. Before they reach the age of eighteen, more than half of our nation's children are likely to spend at least a significant portion of their childhoods living apart from their fathers. Never before in this country have so many children been voluntarily abandoned by their fathers. [iv]

The family is disappearing. The family is becoming a figment of our imagination. Society is slowly erasing the American family. When the family goes, so does the church and all that we believe to be Godly and right. No one is left to build what God has built in His Word – a strong Godly family. It has been said that mothers decide what children believe, but fathers decide what they remember. Think for a moment… if we live in an age void of fathers, it will matter little what mothers teach because there'll be no fathers to create good and lasting memories. What a travesty!

I believe that God protected Noah's family because Noah protected his family. God is a God of linage. The Word clearly builds a picture that Noah lived in wicked times; that men were doing what was wrong and evil in the sight of God. But Noah found favor with the Lord. Noah kept his family out of the cities of filth. Noah and his family lived in a dry deserted place in the desert because Noah cared enough about the safety of his wife and children not to have them live near the danger and corruption of the city. What a good father.

Do you want to survive calamity, build a strong family; take the time necessary to build, nurture, and support the institution of family. Go to church with your children, play with them, sit with them, hug them, talk with them, and go to movies with them. Communicate with them… In the end what matters most – what makes you a real person – is that you have protected and provided for your family.

Family matters to God. If you are upset with your family, fix it; forgive if necessary. Come on, let your mother off the hook; give your father another chance; call your brother; call your sister. Call your parents; tell them how much you appreciate and care about your family. I write this with much compassion regarding my own family. I assure you that every family has to fight to stay a family. There are no special rules for relationships. No matter what, family matters. This is the power of survival.

There is a flipped attitude that we can try out sex without commitment.

Men are spilling their seed without taking on the responsibility of raising the seed they have planted. This is a catastrophe. We have children with no identity. Mothers decide what children believe, fathers decide what they remember. Please, if you are reading this book and you are a father but have not become a daddy to your seed, then start today. Do something!

Divorce is not always the answer!

Make every effort to save your marriage. Do what is necessary to protect it, nurture it, and hold onto it at all cost.

Some tips on building a healthy family life:

1. *Make an attempt to eat dinner at least twice a week together.* I have fond memories of sitting

around the table with my parents growing up. Now, I have two wonderful children... Some of our greatest moments are sitting at the dinner table, laughing and talking about things as a family.

2. *Plan to have a family vacation at least once a year.* Vacations don't have to be a week long, but take some time for the family to hang out.

3. *Have a date night planned out every week.* Take your spouse out. Remember what it was like before kids. Keep the flame alive.

4. *Place God and church as a top priority.* Don't forsake church and youth activities for family time. This gives your child or children the wrong mind set about the things of God.

5. *Tell your spouse daily that you love them.* Let your children hear you. The more you share, care, and love each other, the more secure and happy the children become.

6. *Never destroy each other's spirit.* When you disagree - and you will - stay focused on the disagreement and not on everything else that has happened in times past.

7. *Let your children see you worship and loving on God. Don't be ashamed to lift your hands in church.* Don't be embarrassed to cry when you sense God's presence. This will teach your children more about God than preaching.

8. *Tell your kids you love them daily...* suggest as many times as you can.

9. *Pay your tithes...* teach your kids to pay their tithes...

10. ***Walk in integrity.*** Keep your words. Teach them what truth means.

CHAPTER SEVEN

NOAH WAS A WORSHIPPER

"Then Noah built an altar to the LORD and, taking some of all the clean animals and clean birds, he sacrificed burnt offerings on it. The LORD smelled the pleasing aroma..."
Genesis 8:20-21 NIV

Real Worship is unrehearsed!

The first thing that Noah did was build and altar after exiting the ark. You would think that the first thing Noah wanted to do was run, stretch, and to take a bath since they had no showers and no plumbing. Noah and his entire family had been shut up in a boat with all kinds of smelly animals. But no, he took the time to build an altar! His action reveals a grateful heart. He was thankful!

A THANKFUL HEART IS ALWAYS A FAVORED HEART.

In order to build an altar, Noah had to find the right stones. Then he had to gather wood to build a fire, and Noah didn't possess matches; it took time to build a fire. Noah also needed a sacrifice; he couldn't build an altar without a sacrifice. All this effort and time, why? Because Noah knew if it hadn't been for God, he would have already been defeated. He owed his life, and his entire family's lives to God. God was the reason Noah was still alive and able to build an altar for worship. If you want to survive your worst storm learn how to build an altar.

"Altar" means to slaughter.[v] An altar represents the kind of worship that causes things that are in us to be slaughtered. Things such as anger, bitterness and lust which are keeping us from a holy walk – a right walk – a pure walk with God.

An altar is a raised platform on which you place someone or something as a gift to the Lord.

When you understand the meaning of "altar" you will understand why Noah and other great leaders of the Bible always built altars to the Lord. It's the place where you acknowledge that you are nothing without God. One thing the modern church is missing is the power of the altar. We use to close every sermon with a call to the altar in the old days. Giving people the time to come and lay down

THE SOLE OBJECT OF WORSHIP IS TO ASCRIBE WORTH AND VALUE TO GOD!

their burdens, their sins and their problems. Pastors and leaders would walk around laying hands on people; coming in agreement with them for the release of what was holding them down.

I was raised in the old school kind of church. I wouldn't trade my memories for a million dollars. As a child of Pentecostal background, I grew up watching adults fall on their faces, shouting, praying, crying and lifting their hands to God. This memory has instilled in me the fact that there is more to church than just a sermon. There is an altar! We can come to the altar to lay our burdens down. We can come to the altar the way we are but leave changed.

Noah didn't miss his altar, and God smelled the fragrance of his worship. Do you have a fragrance that attracts God's attention? God smelled Noah's pleasing aroma. Have you given up your altar?

As soon as Abraham gave up his altar he began to lie, trying to protect his own self-interest. When Abraham left his altar, he entered Egypt *(Genesis 20)*. He traded his altar for his comfort, which almost cost him his life. When we lose our altar, we birth **WORSHIP** our Ishmael. The sin of our flesh **UNLOCKS** will produce children. Going to **WEALTH!** church, paying our tithe, and reading our Bible are not our altars. We would like to believe that these necessary acts are our altar, but they are not.

The altar is the place where real worship is offered up to God. Worship requires a sacrifice. Worship requires more than lip service; it requires you. All of you! Worship is the intimate part of your relationship with God. Praise is good, but praise invites God into our presence. God will inhabit the praises of His people, but God doesn't just want to show up. He wants to birth something; He wants to reproduce and multiply. The desire to produce and to take dominion has always been the focus of God for mankind.

> *"And God blessed them, and God said unto them, be fruitful, and multiply, and replenish the earth, and subdue it: and have dominion over the fish of the sea, and over the fowl of the air, and over every living thing that moveth upon the earth." Genesis 1:28*

God desires to plant His spiritual seed in our hearts. Worship moves God past the formalistic ceremonial shout, into the private place of our hearts, where the unclean is slaughtered and replaced with His spiritual seeds of potential and change. God wants to impregnate us with His seed of power, His seed of change, His seed of potential and His seed of destiny. But God will not do this until we learn to build an altar.

Notice what God does right after Noah builds an altar.

"The LORD smelled the pleasing aroma and said in his heart: "Never again will I curse the ground because of man, even though every inclination of his heart is evil from childhood. And never again will I destroy all living creatures, as I have done. As long as the earth endures, seedtime and harvest, cold and heat, summer and winter, day and night will never cease." Then God blessed Noah and his sons, saying to them, "Be fruitful and increase in number and fill the earth." Genesis 8:21-9:1 NIV

God responds to an altar. Notice that Noah's worship had a fragrance that was pleasing to God. When men build an altar, it produces the presence of God to provide a promise or covenant. *Verse nine says that God blessed Noah and his sons*. When a man begins to learn how to

WORSHIP GIVES GOD CHARGE OVER YOUR LIFE!

build and maintain his altar, it affects not only his life, but also his son's life. God gave Noah the same instructions He gave the first man and woman. *"Be fruitful and increase in number and fill the earth."* To be fruitful and to increase seems to be the main thought of the mind of God.

The word "altar" occurs over 350 times in the Bible. The first time it occurs is in Genesis chapter eight, verse twenty, where Noah built an altar. This is also the first time we hear God speak about the covenant of seedtime and harvest. God's focus is the harvest of Noah's willingness to worship with a sacrifice. Worship is a New Testament altar.

NOAH WAS A WORSHIPPER

Not only do you need to build an altar, you must learn how to worship at that altar. The altar is the physical place you establish on which to place your spiritual heart. Worship is proven by what you're willing to walk away from in order to stay in God's presence.

Let me warn you that merely building an altar doesn't necessarily make you a true worshipper. The only person you will be required to please is the Holy Spirit. He's the one person we have ignored in our lives. We must be cautious that we don't grieve the Holy Spirit.

Worship develops in our hearts the ability to approach God, the proper skill of entering into His presence.

Worship is an act born of struggle, as when God called for the offering of Isaac from Abraham. Of course you remember the story... Abraham waited twenty-six long years for Isaac, and after God had supplied the blessing, He asked Abraham to give it back (Genesis 22). Abraham's response has always caught my interest.

> *"And Abraham said to his young men, "Stay here with the donkey; the lad and I will go yonder and worship, and we will come back to you." Genesis 22:5 NKJV*

"The lad and I will go yonder and worship." This is not what God told Abraham to do. He didn't tell him to go to a mountain and worship. God told Abraham to sacrifice Isaac – to sow his son. Abraham must have known something about God that others in his time and age didn't know. He must have known that the seed you sow is seen as worship when it is offered to God.

Worship means more than attending a church service or lifting hands at the direction of a choir leader or pastor. Worship is man's willingness to bow in God's presence and give Him pre-eminence in life. Worship is the place where you step out of the light of the world and into the darkness of His abyss, where God and only God can illuminate you.

The quality of your worship will decide the accuracy of your stone.

King David faced Goliath as a young boy, and He killed

the giant with one stone chosen from a nearby brook. David hit the giant in the temple or forehead which knocked the Goliath down. One stone was able to do the job.

We know David was a man after God's own heart. How was he a man after God's heart? David was a worshipper. Before he was a king... before he was called to the King Saul's table. Before he faced Goliath, David had spent hours worshipping God.

FACTS ABOUT WORSHIP:

- *Worship produces the power to overcome any storm.*
- *Worship provides us with the impartation of God's seed.*
- *Worship goes far deeper into the presence of God than praise.*
- *Worship starts in the heart, and makes its way to the surface of our lives by our lifestyle.*
- *Worship creates access to God.*
- *Worship builds peace in the atmosphere.*
- *Worship produces joy.*
- *Worship allows the heart to release its cares.*
- *Worship builds a better mind set for Godly living.*
- *Real worship is deadly to the enemy.*
- *God's power is released in worship.*
- *Healing can take place while you are worshipping.*
- *Lifted hands in worship allow others to see your surrendered heart.*

CHAPTER EIGHT

NOAH WAS ABLE TO SUCCEED IN SPITE OF GREAT CRITICISM

"When on life's journey it becomes our lot to travel with criticism of skeptics, the hate of some, the rejection of others, the impatience of many, or a friend's betrayal, we must be able to pray in such a manner that an abiding faith and a strong testimony that the Lord will be with us to the end, will compel us to say, "Nevertheless, Father, Thy will be done, and with Thy help, in patience I will follow firmly on the path that takes me back to Thee." Angel Abrea[vi]

One thing I have learned in life. Never live for the opinions of others. Here are the facts.

- *Haters are going to hate.*
- *Judgers are going to judge*
- *Critics are going to criticize.*

It doesn't pay to live for the opinions of others. The most miserable day in your life is when you decide to live your life the way others believe you should. The most joyous day will be when you decide to only live your life to please God. When God gives you an instruction it will usually cause those around you to become frustrated with you.

Imagine for a moment... God gives you an instruction and that instruction is far from what you have ever seen. God told Noah to build an ark, but why? Because it was going to rain; but what was rain? Up to this point in man's history man had never seen rain; *for a mist would come up from the ground and water the earth.*

We already know that the people of Noah's time were wicked and self-centered for their own pleasure and gain. It might be safe to say that the people around Noah weren't going to receive the message that it would rain.

> *"Now the earth was corrupt in God's sight and was full of violence. God saw how corrupt the earth had become, for all the people on earth had corrupted their ways. So God said to Noah, "I am going to put an end to all people, for the earth is filled with violence because of them. I am surely going to destroy both them and the earth. So make yourself an ark of cypress wood; make rooms in it and coat it with pitch inside and out..." Genesis 6:11-14 NIV*

How long would it take Noah to build a colossal ship? I wonder how many years Noah had to endure people's insults. People probably walked up to him asking questions. He might have answered, "I'm building an Ark because it's going to rain." They may have asked him about rain, and why he was doing what he was doing.

Noah might have answered, "God is going to destroy the world and so He has commanded me to build this Ark. Do you want to repent from your wicked ways and go with me?" It seems likely that the people just walked away and laughed because the only humans on the Ark were Noah and his family.

"Any fool can criticize, condemn, and complain... and most fools do..." Dale Carnegie[vii]

You are going to have to survive the criticism of those who don't understand your assignment if you plan on doing anything for God. Others will *criticize* you when they don't understand what you are about.

Criticism is the death gargle of non-achievers.

If you are going to survive the cesspool of those who are not for you, you better be confident in who you are. Let me give you a few keys for walking through crowds of those who aren't for you.

HOW TO SURVIVE YOUR CRITICS:

1. *You must have a secure identity.*
2. *You must have a clear picture of what you are all about.*
3. *You must know exactly what your assignment is.*
4. *You can't rummage through your past expecting to enter your future.*
5. *You must realize that any attempt to obey God will produce enemies all along the way.*
6. *Remember, a critic is someone who judges others because it reminds them of what they are not doing.*

Noah had to work by day and preach by night that God was going to flood the earth and destroy anyone who was not in the Ark. Every day he worked and preached, but no one offered to help. No one repented. When the time came to get into the Ark, no one came to enter its safety. The way you get through a storm is to stay focused on God. Don't let those who are judging over you discourage you. God will do what He said He will do.

If you are planning to live a life void of criticism, then you best make plans right now to do nothing, say nothing and attempt to be nothing. The proof that you are on the right road is usually someone telling you that you are not.

I like what Bishop T.D. Jakes once said, *"When men are praising you, just keep on walking... when they are criticizing you, just keep on walking."* If you want to survive the rat race, you must stay away from the rats. Close your ears to any other voice but God's voice.

"It is not the critic who counts; not the man who points out how the strong man stumbles, or where the doer of deeds could have done them better. The credit belongs to the man who is actually in the arena, whose face is marred by dust and sweat and blood; who strives valiantly... who errs, who comes short again and again... who knows great enthusiasms, the great devotions; who spends himself in a worthy cause, who at best knows in the end the triumph of high achievement, and who at the worst, if he fails, at least fails while

daring greatly, so that his place shall never be with those cold and timid souls who know neither victory nor defeat." Theodore Roosevelt[viii]

Criticism is when someone is watching your faults and decides to judge them. Any time you attempt to do what God has called you to do, expect your critics to show up and judge what you are doing. I once heard someone say that if you want to discover your enemies announce your goals. When you awaken your assignment, you will also awaken your enemy.

Noah obviously had critics. Out of all the people who lived around Noah, only his immediate family was present with him in the Ark. If you plan to succeed in anything, you will have to endure your critics…

FACTS ABOUT CRITICISM:

- *Criticism is one of the signs that promotion is around the corner.*
- *People who criticize you are convinced your goals are achievable.*
- *People criticize what they don't understand.*
- *Criticism is the death gargle of a non-achiever.*
- *Criticism is the sign of insecurity.*
- *Critics are necessary for positive growth to take place.*

CHAPTER NINE

NOAH BELIEVED IN THE POWER OF THE SEED

"NOAH, A MAN OF THE SOIL, PROCEEDED TO PLANT A VINEYARD..." GENESIS 9:20 NIV

The most dangerous word to the enemy is the word **SEED**. I believe this one word terrifies the devil and sends fear running down his spine.

I began to unfold the meaning of *resource* and *provision* in chapter six. I want to dig further into the subject of the seed. I can trace most, perhaps all, of my increase to the power of sowing a seed.

Noah received the same command that God had given Adam and Eve after he built **ONE OF THE MOST DANGEROUS WORDS IN THE BIBLE IS SEED!** an altar. *"Be fruitful and multiply"* (Genesis (9:1). If we are to multiply in this world, we are going to have to sow a seed. If you want to have children, sow your seed. If you want to have produce, sow a seed. Seed-time and harvest is the greatest law that God has given man, and it's the one law we don't want to talk about in nominal churches.

> *"Again Jesus began to teach by the lake. The crowd that gathered around him was so large that he got into a boat and sat in it out on the lake, while all the people were along the shore at the water's edge. He taught them many things by parables, and in his teaching said: "Listen! A farmer went out to sow his seed." Mark 4:1-3 NIV*

Notice what Jesus said after He gave the parable of sowing.

"...The secret of the kingdom of God has been given to you..." Mark 4:11 NIV

"Then Jesus said to them, "Don't you understand this parable? How then will you understand any parable?" Mark 4:13 NIV

If we don't study and understand the law of sowing, we could be missing the secrets of the Kingdom. Jesus said that if we understand the parable of the sower then we would understand the rest of the parables as well.

It was God's plan that we should be seed sowers. Whenever I use the term *seed sower*, most people pay attention. But when I announce that *money* is the seed, many try to shut me out, but money seeds will produce a money harvest.

One question that haunts people in church is whether they can sow seed to expect increase if they're not living right. My answer to that is yes. The principle of harvest is not based on your lifestyle. Harvest is based on sowing; however, do I believe that you're blessed just because you have experienced a financial harvest? NO, I do not. The blessings of God go far beyond finances. They move in realms of peace of mind, a good home, a secure life, health, children walking in protection, and curses being lifted from your house; all of which are more than just the result of sowing. They are the results of an obedient life to God's Word.

Never assume that because you are experiencing increase God is in approval of your lifestyle. It's possible to have financial increase and not be spiritually okay. Hear my heart; I desire to be in good standing with both. But if I had to choose, I'd rather be in favor with God than have all the money in the world. God can replace what man cannot. It is better to do what is right in the eyes of the Lord than to have all the money you need.

The terms *sowing* and *reaping* stump so many in nominal churches. Maybe it's not so much the sowing and reaping that stumps them, but the idea that we sow expecting God to get involved in it. God brings the increase. After Noah built an altar, God made a covenant that seed-time and harvest would never cease. It is obvious that after worship God's focus turns to sowing and reaping. (Genesis 8:22)

One of the greatest books I've read that changed my mindset on giving was, "*31 Reasons People Don't Have a Financial Harvest,*" written by Dr. Mike Murdock. Allow me to tell you a story about my life.

I was pastoring a church, preaching about the *blessings of God* while I was *financially broke*. My wife drove an Aerostar van, in which neither the heat nor the air conditioner worked. I remember standing in the parking lot of our apartment complex one cold morning, watching my wife and my two children drive off to school. It was winter in North Carolina, and my family was bundled up in coats, gloves and toboggans. They knew that the car's heater didn't work. My heart sank! I drove off in my messed up pub pickup with tears running down my face. I prayed a prayer that changed my life forever. *I began to ask God why I was so financially broke; what was wrong with me? I believed in the blessings of God... I preached them from the pulpit, but I was living a life of lack. I kept praying...asking, "Lord have I offended you? Are you angry with me?"* The answer I received wasn't the answer I was looking for. *"Son, you're missing my law of financial increase."*

I was walking through a local bookstore later that same day, searching for information that would change my life. After a few minutes, I looked up and sitting on the book-shelf was the very answer I had been praying for that morning, *"31 Reasons People Don't Receive Their Financial Harvest,"* by Mike Murdock.

GOD HAS HIDDEN YOUR PROVISION IN THE POWER OF YOUR RESOURCES

I could hardly believe my eyes. The thought that was racing through my mind was... *I remember Mike Murdock. He used to come to our church when I was a young boy.* I picked up the last copy of this book from the shelf, handed it to the sales clerk and waited as she tried to scan it three times. She looked at me and said, "Sir, we don't sell Mike Murdock books here." I couldn't believe it! I told her that I had found that book on the shelf. She explained that she couldn't scan it because it was not in the store's system. I picked up the book and noticed the publisher's price tag of $12.00 on the cover. I asked the sales clerk if she could sell me the book for the price printed on the cover. She did, and I left that day with the book that would change my life.

To this day, that bookstore does not sell any of Mike Murdock's books. I ran to my office opened the book, and this is what I read…

"The only cure for confusion is the Wisdom of God… Every parent needs money. Every minister is worthy of abundant finances… You will never be the same again after reading this book. Here is your own prosperity handbook… Too many people are hurting… too many people are hungry… too many people are ignorant and too many people are poor. Prosperity is having enough of Divine provision to complete a Divine Assignment. YOU CAN PROSPER. YOU MUST PROSPER. YOU WILL PROSPER!" (Paraphrased)[ix]

I began to devour the information that was written. I not only read it, but I began to apply the information in my life. When I began to tithe properly, and to sow my seeds for a desired result, finances began to show up. Not right away, but through the process of change. As my wife and I applied God's laws and principles of increase we began to experience change. God began to honor our efforts and increase started flowing.

Let me give you two words that helped me. ***Resource***

and **Provision.** Abraham coined the phrase *"Jehovah Jireh, the Lord is my supplier (Genesis 22:14)."*

Resource means something that lies ready for use; it could be money, property, assets, or potential.[x]

Provision means something provided, prepared, or supplied for the future; a preparatory arrangement or measure taken in advance for meeting a future need.[xi]

Discoveries create opportunities. When you walk with God, He will open your mind so that you will discover the resources that have been hidden around you. God placed everything in the Earth that it would need when He created it. This is what we call resources. For example, gold is hidden in the earth until someone is willing to take the time and effort to look, dig or pan for it. The gold will stay hidden in the earth until the dirt is removed, and it's worth is uncovered (at this time about $542.00 per ounce). The hidden resource of **gold** can become provision.

There has to be a power of discovery. Discovery is the doorway to opportunity. Aerodynamics has always existed. The power and ability to fly had already been encoded in the resources of the earth, but no one could fly until the law of aerodynamics was discovered. When the resource of flying was exposed, the provision of that law was also exposed. Now we can travel in one day what once would have taken a lifetime.

Within the resources of your life are the hidden secrets of your provision. Remember, provision is something provided, prepared or supplied in advance for your future. There's something hidden in your present that, if discovered, will open the door to your future.

The seed you're holding contains the hidden secret of its power that God has spoken over it. Hidden in your seed is the power of provision. The seed in your hand is the resource that will produce your future provision.

You can count the seeds in a watermelon, but you can't count the watermelons in a seed. Only God knows what resources have been encoded in the seed. Until you are willing to plant a seed, you will never discover the power that has been pre-arranged in it. The seed is the resource that awaits your movement of faith to sow it, to uncover its harvest potential. Provision is provided for the person who discovers the power of a seed.

The seed is the resource that God has placed around you, and the provision of your future hides in that seed. God has already prepared this seed in advance to create what is needed for increase. God is the only one who knows what has been spoken into that seed. So when God impresses you to sow, it's not the seed that has His attention, but the secret message that has been hidden within it. You and I will never discover the power of a seed until we let it die.

"Verily, verily, I say unto you, except a corn of wheat fall into the ground and die, it abideth

alone: but if it dies, it bringeth forth much fruit." John 12:24

Stop keeping alive what God's been trying to kill! The seed that stays on the shelf will never produce food for the farmer. If fruit didn't fall from a tree, rot and die, its seeds would never be exposed. Death is the process for something else to live. Loss can produce gain when God gets involved in it. When you learn the law of reciprocity, which means the law of mutual exchange, you'll begin to supply your life with increase. Whatever you do, don't ignore the power of sowing and reaping. Plant your seeds, and expect them to produce a wonderful harvest for you. Let me give you my formula.

- **SATAN SUBTRACTS**
- **MAN DIVIDES**
- **GOD MULTIPLIES**

When you let go of your seed to build the Kingdom of God, God will release from that seed the power to multiply. When you place that same seed into the hand of the enemy, he will begin to subtract its power from your life. When you let seeds stay in your hand, you can only divide them.

CHAPTER TEN

NOAH POSSESSED INCREDIBLE PATIENCE

"The LORD is good unto them that wait for him, to the soul that seeketh him. It is good that a man should both hope and quietly wait for the salvation of the LORD."
Lamentations 3:25-26

"Nothing gives one person so much advantage over another as to remain always cool and unruffled under all circumstances." Thomas Jefferson[xii]

The name "Noah" means rest or quite.[xiii] Think about how long it must have taken Noah to accomplish this one instruction to build an Ark. He had to gather all the materials and then undergo a task that he had never seen or known. All Noah had were the blueprints that God had given him.

DO WHAT IS PRACTICAL; GOD WILL DO WHAT IS SUPERNATURAL

Noah carried the burden of knowing that the completion of this task meant the doom of all mankind and creatures alike, while he was making way on God's instruction. Mankind was to be punished. All those not entering the Ark with him would die.

Noah was truly a man of patience and rest. To be able to carry such a burden without collapsing, to be able to accomplish God's entire plan without hesitation or complaint, reveals a quality of patience. Patience doesn't just mean that you have the ability to wait on something. Patience is when you can wait and not complain about how long it's taking. Patience is being stable and keeping your endurance while you wait.

"My brethren, count it all joy when ye fall into

84

divers temptations; Knowing this, that the trying of your faith worketh **patience**. *But* **let patience have her perfect work***, that ye may be perfect and entire, wanting nothing. If any of you lack wisdom, let him ask of God, that giveth to all men liberally, and upbraideth not; and it shall be given him." James 1:2-5*

The Greek meaning for *"patience"* in this passage is *to have a cheerful or hopeful endurance, or constancy.*[xiv]

Patience produces perfect work... When we are patient we can wait on what we want without losing our cheerfulness and hopefulness in the process. We maintain our joy no matter how long it takes. God can't use anyone who doesn't possess the ability to cheerfully wait. Think about it, most everything that we get from God comes after much toiling and waiting.

"Behold, we count them happy which endure. Ye have heard of the patience of Job, and have seen the end of the Lord; that the Lord is very pitiful, and of tender mercy." James 5:11

Job had to endure much loss and sadness. Even in his worst condition, when the trials that surrounded him were invading his person, he maintained enough sense not to lose his patience. How did Job keep his grip on his emotions and not lose his patience? *Job 19:25 says,* **"For I know that my redeemer liveth, and that he shall stand at the latter day upon the earth..."** Job kept his perspective – he never lost his faith in his God. He knew as long as his Redeemer lived, there was hope for a turnaround. He knew that God was able – more than enough – to do the supernatural. Job knew this and so did Noah. We must do the practical; God will do the supernatural! Job, Noah and the other patriarchs all possessed incredible faith to believe no matter how long they had to wait. They possessed the power of patience.

Let me give you a formula that will help you:

1. *Don't lose your perspective; it will cost you your point of view.*

2. *Problems are a part of life. So stop telling God how big your problems are, and start telling your problems how BIG YOUR GOD IS!*

3. *If you fail to elevate yourself in worship you will stagnate in your crisis.*

4. *Patience is waiting for a desired result and never losing focus that it's on the way.*

Faith is not enough...

"And beside this, giving all diligence, add to your faith virtue; and to virtue knowledge; And to knowledge temperance; and to temperance patience; and to patience godliness; And to godliness brotherly kindness; and to brotherly kindness charity." 2 Peter 1:5-7

You must, with all diligence, add to your faith *virtue*, which is moral excellence or doing the right things. Add to your virtue *knowledge*, **which** is the power of information, and add to your knowledge *temperance*, which means self-restraint. Then you must add to your temperance *patience*, and to patience *godliness*, and to godliness *brotherly kindness*, and to kindness *charity*, which is love, meaning also *to give*. Notice that there is so much more to this walk with God than just confessing your belief system.

Patience produces hope...

> *"And not only so, but we glory in tribulations also: knowing that tribulation worketh patience; And patience, experience; and experience, hope: And hope maketh not ashamed; because the love of God is shed abroad in our hearts by the Holy Ghost which is given unto us." Romans 5:3-5*

Patience gives us the time to live through and survive the tribulations of life so that we can gain experience. Experience produces hope. How? By living through distressful situations which otherwise should have or could have killed us. As you survive your tribulation, you develop one powerful message. I understand that what you've been through has embarrassed you at times, but I've got good news, in the end you'll no longer be ashamed.

Patience is the ability to stand on a promise when everything around you is telling you to give up, to accept your lot in life. It does not matter how long you've been waiting for your healing – don't give up! Don't let time weaken your faith! On the contrary – stay focused! Stay joyous! Stay cheerful! Your harvest is on the way! The difference between a mosquito blessing and an elephant blessing is time. Mosquito eggs can hatch in three days[xv]; babies in seven days; an elephant is pregnant almost two whole years![xvi]

> *"For we are saved by hope: but hope that is seen is not hope: for what a man seeth, why doth he yet hope for? But if we hope for that we see not, then do we with patience wait for it. Likewise the Spirit also helpeth our infirmities: for we know not what we should pray for as we ought: but the Spirit itself maketh intercession for us with groanings which cannot be uttered. And he that searcheth the hearts knoweth what is the mind of the Spirit, **because he maketh intercession for the saints according to the will of God.** And we know that all things work together for good to them that love God, to them who are the called according to his purpose." Romans 8:24-28*

I've often vowed that I'm not going to pray for patience, knowing that patience comes only through trials. However, it doesn't matter what you pray, trials are a part of everyday living. Whether you pray for patience or not, you will have to live through trials.

Patience proves your calling….

> *"But in all things approving ourselves as the ministers of God, in much patience, in afflictions, in necessities, in distresses," 2 Corinthians 6:4*

Patience proves that you are walking worthy of the Lord…

> *"That ye might walk worthy of the Lord unto all pleasing, being fruitful in every good work, and increasing in the knowledge of God; Strengthened with all might, according to his glorious power, unto all patience and longsuffering with joyfulness;" Colossians 1:10-11*

Patience produces your miracle…

> *"That ye be not slothful, but followers of them who through faith and patience inherit the promises." Hebrews 6:12*

Acquiring patience will help you to produce your harvest and your miracle. Waiting is the process by which all increase and wealth travels. The Bible often admonishes us to not become weary. The weariness of the believer has weakened the twenty-first century church. We have lost our patience, and in return, we have lost our faith and joy; which has produced a crumbling, complaining church.

Patience produces strength to outlast the storm...

> *"But they that wait upon the LORD shall renew their strength; they shall mount up with wings as eagles; they shall run, and not be weary; and they shall walk, and not faint." Isaiah 40:31*

Don't become weary in well doing, for in due season you will reap if you do not faint (Galatians 6:9 paraphrased)!

To survive and thrive again in any crisis takes patience to trust and believe the Word of God! Noah did, and he and his entire family survived to thrive again!

CHAPTER ELEVEN

NOAH WAS ABLE TO SUCCEED IN SPITE OF GREAT OPPOSITION

Opposition is merely an opportunity in disguise.

So many people have succeeded in life in spite of facing some of the greatest opposition imaginable. No one will ever thrive from a crisis unless they are willing to perceive it with a different mindset.

THERE ARE NO CERTAINTIES IN LIFE; ONLY OPPORTUNITIES

Ask yourself whether the crisis you're facing is a problem or a promotion? Pastor Clint Brown, a friend of mine, preached on this very subject at the Favor Center Church. He asked this question… "Is what you are a facing a problem or could it be a promotion?"

A problem is a promotion awaiting its discovery.

Noah was able to *survive to thrive* because he was able to endure and walk through great opposition.

NOAH WAS ALONE IN HIS TASK.

It's obvious to me that Noah had to accomplish his assignment alone without much support from his immediate family. If you expect to be at the top, expect to be there alone. Solitude can be your greatest asset in times of growth and increase.

Consider this. Noah preached and preached about the coming rain and that the Ark was not just for him and his family but for all who wanted to escape the coming judgment of the Lord. But when the time came, no one came into the Ark to enter its safety. Noah was alone with his family.

Your assignment will usually appear irrational and illogical to others.

Imagine being given an assignment and a message that no one responds to, that no one helps fulfill and that no one encourages. I'm sure that Noah was the talk of the town. He was probably the laughing stock in the taverns; the grey-headed old man building some ungodly looking building in the middle of a desert; calling it a boat for something called rain. What a crazy old fool they must have thought him to be.

Watch out for the voice of discouragement when fulfilling your God given assignment.

I'm sure that Noah's wife doubted him on more than one occasion, told him how his children were being teased both at school and at work, how embarrassed they felt about his project. Perhaps she even questioned him, *"Noah, are you sure? Are you sure that God told you that this catastrophe is really coming?"*

I have found in over twenty-five years of ministry that most of what we do for God we will first have to do alone You will have to possess an incredible amount of faith in God, and in your own assurance that God has really spoken to you. I've had to experience this myself quite often. I've had to be able to preach to my own faith; lay hands on my own head. I've had to look in the mirror to assure myself that I was going to make it! People who are going to do extraordinary things for God need to be aware that they may have to go alone at first.

I couldn't imagine preaching for years and having no one respond, no one attend, and no one come to the altar. I wonder if I could have stayed motivated to continue my task. I wonder if I could have done what Noah did. I hope I could have. This I know for sure, God does His best work when we are all alone. In the secret place of our pain God shows up to do His greatest surgery.

NOAH HAD NO PRIOR SKILLS OR KNOWLEDGE IN REGARD TO SHIPBUILDING.

God loves to choose people who are not qualified for the endeavor He assigns them to do. I believe God does this to exercise their faith, while He also keeps them dependent upon Him.

We will be more apt to listen and to learn when we set out to accomplish what we have no knowledge of completing. God loves to qualify the unqualified. He loves to call the unlearned and mentor them to their greatness.

I am convinced that when you set your heart to work for God, you will start with very little knowledge of what He has called you to do. God wants to humble you. He wants you to pray and study for the task you are to fulfill. He calls the weak and anoints them to do great exploits.

> *"... but the people that do know their God shall be strong, and do exploits."* Daniel 11:32

NOAH DID NOT KNOW WHAT RAIN WAS...

Noah lacked the proper knowledge of what he was assigned to do. This is where God uses our faith rather than our intellect to accomplish our task. God gave Noah a glimpse of what was coming. Noah only envisioned what God saw but had no idea what it was. He had never seen rain. Up to this point in man's history God would let a mist fall on the ground to water the earth, but it had never rained. Water had never fallen from the sky. Noah was faced with having to explain this new phenomenon to others; although he himself did not yet comprehend it. When Noah had to explain rain, he may have said, "Yes, this seems a bit far out!" When asked how he could know about these things, Noah probably answered, "Because GOD TOLD ME." They must have thought him crazy!

NOAH LACKED THE PROPER TOOLS...

Just because you lack the proper tools doesn't mean you are exempt from the task. This is where you have to become creative. To thrive in life you may have to learn how to use things that would unmistakably be used for something else. Don't stay in the box that others have dictated for you. Think outside of the box. No, better yet, throw away the box!

NOAH HAD TO BECOME THE FIRST ZOO KEEPER...

Nowhere in the Bible do we find Noah having the skills to be a zookeeper. God was not only going to fill the Ark with people; God was also going to put animals in the Ark – two by two – male and female.

> *"There went in two and two unto Noah into the ark, the male and the female, as God had commanded Noah." Genesis 7:9*

When God is looking for someone to fulfill His purpose, He has to find someone who is willing to be inconvenienced for the sake of fulfilling His plan. This doesn't sound like the ministry we see today does it? We have attempted to make the things of God easy and compliant for the people instead of making the people more compliant for God.

Where in the entire Bible do we find God concerned about making people comfortable with Him? It is my opinion that we should never get too comfortable with God. God emphatically lets us know where wisdom begins. To fear the Lord is the beginning of WISDOM (Proverbs 9:10)! Fearing God is healthy!

NOAH HAD NO MENTOR TO SEEK COUNSEL FROM...

Noah had a huge task to take on, with no one to call, and no one to seek counsel from. There were no shipbuilders. There was no other person who had successfully survived a similar crisis from which Noah could glean some insight. No, Noah had to rely solely on the Word of God.

There were no bookstores to which Noah could retreat to read about others who had survived to thrive again. There were no manuals on how to nurture and care for animals. Noah had to trust every decision that he made to be the right decision.

If you plan to succeed in any area of your life, you will most likely have to do it through opposition. Dr. Murdock has often said to me that adversaries decide rewards.

If David had never faced and defeated Goliath, he would have never found the doorway into the palace. Others saw a giant and a problem, but David saw an opportunity. Let me interject that God never told David to fight Goliath. David turned an opposition into an opportunity. He faced his problem and turned it into a promotion.

God didn't just create you to survive crises. He made you to succeed in them – to thrive. What God did for people like Noah, Job, David and Abraham He will do for you.

Survive to Thrive

CHAPTER TWELVE

REACTIONS DECIDE ACTION!

*Your Reactions speak louder to God
than your praise...*

There is no day immune from possibly receiving bad news or experiencing something that externally seems to be undefeatable. Our external world is constantly evolving and changing. We are powerless to stop things that happen around us; yet we can be full of power internally which will give us the ability to ensure that our internal world doesn't change in a wrong way.

Everything that is happening around you is revealing what is happening in you.

"Circumstances don't make us; they reveal us."

All the enemy has to do to see what you are becoming is turn up the heat externally; what comes out of you will reveal the real you. The storm shows the enemy and those around us who we are and what we are made of.

Life without conflict or crisis would be a life without rewards and advancement. When **WHAT YOU SAY DECIDES WHAT YOU FEEL.** God wants to bless us, He assigns an enemy to us. The size of your enemy determines the size of your reward. We have to understand that the enemy is not always a person; it can be a major crisis or a circumstance. Your test will most likely come in a way you are not looking for it.

There are so many ways the storm can come; a child not doing what is expected, a spouse not performing or living up to their commitments or a job that stops your promotion. Maybe you didn't get the money you thought you were supposed to get on your next pay day. Let's face it, life is full of disappointments. I bet you can think of things right now that have happened that you thought you would never make it through. But look at you, you survived! You made it! Oh, you may have cried, you may have hurt deeply in your spirit, but you survived. You are still alive. You are still here.

The devil should have killed you while he had you. Now your faith is rising up, and you are going to walk in your season of success and favor.

Reactions are deadly. Your reactions are the only source that leaks information to the outside world of what is going on in the inside world.

Jesus appeared many times to prove he had resurrected after his death. I believe there were at least three times He appeared to deal with wrong reactions; reactions that could have cost the early leaders and eventually the church's failure. I've chosen this last chapter to specifically deal with our reactions.

Reactions can cause great trouble in our future.

REACTION OF FEAR:

The disciples experienced the storm of a lifetime. They watched their leader, Jesus, get arrested, beaten, jailed and crucified until he was dead. They believed His body had been stolen and that they were the next in line to experience the same punishment.

> *"Then, the same day at evening, being the first day of the week, when the **doors were shut where the disciples were assembled, for fear of the Jews**, Jesus came and stood in the midst, and said to them, "Peace be with you." When He had said this, He showed them His hands and His side. Then the disciples were glad when they saw the Lord. So Jesus said to them again, "Peace to you! As the Father has sent Me, I also send you." And when He had said this, He breathed on them, and said to them, "Receive the Holy Spirit. If you forgive the sins of any, they are forgiven them; if you retain the sins of any, they are retained."*
> *John 20:19-23 NKJV*

Jesus stood in the middle of them and declared a season of peace. He said, "Peace be with you."

WHAT YOU SAY DECIDES WHAT YOU BELIEVE

The disciples had assembled because of fear. They didn't assemble to have a prayer meeting and encourage one another on how to be committed to the cause. They didn't get together to discuss their warfare strategies on how to defeat the enemy. They were gathered in hiding because they were afraid.

This is a normal response after such a major storm. The experience and pain of loss is sometimes almost unbearable. When our last attempt at something fails it creates a memory of pain, loss and defeat. These memories can keep us from moving into our future. The inability to release those memories will create a season of fear, and fear always produces cowards. Fear stops us from confronting what needs to be changed. Fear paralyzes us from kicking down the walls that have imprisoned us and keeps us from believing for something better.

What were the disciples really afraid of? I believe they were afraid of the unknown. Someone once said the disciples were afraid to die. I don't believe that. Most of these men died for what they believed. But the unknown; not knowing what to expect next; thinking that all you've done and worked for is gone. Now that will create fear.

Fear is a deadly reaction when not dealt with. Fear in itself is not evil. Fear can be used to make sure that your movement is properly lined up. The Bible says that to fear the Lord is the beginning of wisdom. Not all fear is evil fear. Fear is a built-in warning that something may not fit or be right. However, fear stopping you from breaking free and paralyzing you from living a victorious life is fear is sent by the enemy.

> *"For God has not given us a spirit of fear, but of power and of love and of a sound mind." 2 Timothy 1:7 NKJV*

A reaction of fear is deadly. Let's call this fear worry. The disciples were sitting in the room worrying about what was going to happen next.

Worry is confidence in your adversary... Faith is confidence is God.

Let me give you the remedy for fear...

1. **Be convinced of who the Lord is...**

   "The LORD is my light and my salvation; whom shall I fear? The LORD is the strength of my life; of whom shall I be afraid?" Psalm 27:1

2. **Rest in the fact that God is going to deal with your enemy...**

   "When the wicked, even mine enemies and my foes, came upon me to eat up my flesh, they stumbled and fell." Psalm 27:2

3. **Do not lose your confidence when those around you have mounted up to make war against you.**

   "Though an host should encamp against me, my heart shall not fear: though war should rise against me, in this will I be confident." Psalm 27:3

4. **Make the house of God your focus and be committed to serve in your local church.**

   "One thing have I desired of the LORD, that will I seek after; that I may dwell in the house of the LORD all the days of my life, to behold the beauty of the LORD, and to inquire in his temple." Psalm 27:4

5. **God will hide you in His secret place where the enemy has no access.**

   "For in the time of trouble he shall hide me in his pavilion: in the secret of his tabernacle shall he hide me; he shall set me up upon a rock." Psalm 27:5

6. **You will be raised above your enemies. God will cause you to be a success.**

   "And now shall mine head be lifted up above mine enemies round about me: therefore will I offer in his tabernacle sacrifices of joy; I will sing, yea, I will sing praises unto the LORD." Psalm 27:6

REACTION OF UNBELIEF:

Fear can be one of the most dangerous reactions, but this next one can stop every blessing and miracle that was scheduled to your life.

"The other disciples therefore said unto him, we have seen the Lord. But he said unto them, except I shall see in his hands the print of the nails, and put my finger into the print of the nails, and thrust my hand into his side, I will not believe." John 20:25

Unbelief is a reaction that will stop every blessing that has been sent your way. Psalms 68:19 says that God loads us down daily with benefits or blessings. I asked the Lord, *"Daily?"*

God spoke to me, *"Everyday I'm sending blessings and miracles toward you and past you."*

What's the problem? I haven't been receiving any miracles.

The only problem is that we are unable to see them. I believe that the reason most Christians haven't yet experienced the miracle hand of God is for lack of faith and unbelief.

Thomas said he wouldn't believe unless he saw it with his own eyes. Now, this is strange because these were his friends. They were men of honor, not accustomed to lying; yet he wouldn't believe them. Unbelief caused Jesus to walk through the wall and appear to Thomas.

"And after eight days again his disciples were within, and Thomas with them: then came

Jesus, the doors being shut, and stood in the midst, and said, Peace be unto you. Then saith he to Thomas, reach hither thy finger, and behold my hands; and reach hither thy hand, and thrust it into my side: and be not faithless, but believing." John 20:26-27

Jesus appeared and showed Thomas his scars.

Jesus appears to deal with unbelief. Unbelief will place delay on your promise. I believe that one of God's pains is to be doubted and one of His greatest pleasures is to be believed. Doubt causes great pain because it hinders and places limits on a limitless God. Imagine being able to do anything...having all power... never ever being wrong. Now imagine being able to do or accomplish anything, except that your power is attached to someone else. Someone has to believe you can do what you know you can do in order for you to perform. What are you going to do? The same thing God does. You are going to try every way possible to get someone to see your power.

Faith is the force that releases into our dimension what God has already released in His. Unbelief will completely destroy what God has planned on doing. This is why I believe that Jesus showed up to deal with Thomas and stop the enemy of unbelief.

Why aren't we receiving and experiencing all of God's goodness? Many simply don't believe.

FORMULA FOR MANIFESTATION:

1. <u>ASK</u>
- We have not because we ask not, and when we ask we ask a miss. (James 4:3)
- Questions are the only bosses answers will respond to.
- Answers are around us every day waiting for the question to reveal them.

2. <u>ANSWER</u>
- God always answers immediately.

> *"Then said unto me, fear not, Daniel: **for from the first day that** thou didst set thine heart to understand and to chasten thyself before thy God, thy words were heard, and I am come for thy words."* Daniel 10:12

3. <u>RECEIVING</u>
- Get in alignment for the entry of your blessing.

Let me ask you a question. **Have you taken advantage of everything the Word of God says you can have?** The greatest battle over your faith will be in your mind. God uses faith. By faith we know that the worlds were framed by the Word of God (Hebrews 11:3).

Faith attached to words is the creative power and source that creates your world. God looked out into nothing, with His faith spoke and there it was. He hung the sun and all we see by the power of His spoken words. The Word of God declares that God has hidden His treasures in earthen vessels (II Corinthians 4:7). I believe that treasure is Jesus and that through Jesus we have the power of faith to speak and create our world. We can reframe our world by faith. Don't like your world? Change your faith.

- *God only responds to our faith.*
- *Faith decides divine timing. Faith is expectation of your harvest.*
- *I can know your faith level but what you say.*
- *If others aren't talking to your faith, then you talk to it.*

You can be, or do and have anything you want if you would just work your faith. Mental barriers will stop God's blessings. **Trust gives faith its' life.** Barrier is defined as a thing that prevents passage or approach; obstruction.[xvii]

SIX MENTAL BARRIES:

1. Fear that it will never happen.
2. Mental images that create false imaginations.
3. The opinion of others. Allow the wounds from others to heal.
4. Past experiences. The hurting become master menders.
5. Stubborn mentality that stops you from learning and changing.
6. Mental limitations. You are your worst enemy.

God's plan is to give us peace. Peace that transcends wisdom. Peace that passes all understanding. There is a place in God that the mind can't go; only the heart of faith is allowed to enter. Remember, the mind and the intellect are attached to the flesh. Faith is attached to the heart of believing. There is a place in your next season where you have to trust and not understand (Proverbs 3:5-6). Step where you can't see; sing when you feel defeated. The enemy is watching your faith, and hell has no understanding of faith. Hell is watching your posture. Your posture is attached to your faith. Your faith is attached to the power of God's Word.

REACTION OF BACKSLIDING:

Backsliding is a reaction that stops forward progression.

Another time Jesus appeared was when Peter decided to go back to fishing. I believe once again Jesus was dealing with a problem. The problem is reacting the same way we used to react when things don't go the way we want them to go. The old church use to call it *backsliding.*

> *"Simon Peter said to them, "I am going fishing." They said to him, "We are going with you also." They went out and immediately got into the boat, and that night they caught nothing. but when the morning had now come, Jesus stood on the shore; yet the disciples did not know that it was Jesus. Then Jesus said to*

*them, "Children, have you any food?" They
answered Him, "No..." Therefore that disciple
whom Jesus loved said to Peter, "It is the
Lord!" Now when Simon Peter heard that it
was the Lord, he put on his outer garment (for
he had removed it), and plunged into the sea."
John 21:3-5 7 NKJV*

Notice that when Peter decided to go back fishing, all the others decided to go with him. Most of the disciples weren't fishermen. When we decide to back up we have no idea who will be backing up with us. Backsliding is contagious.

Backsliding is when God moves and we don't.

God cannot use anyone who keeps falling back into his old nature and ways. Those who are always looking back aren't fit for the kingdom of God (Luke 9:62). Why? They never pass the test. They are always trying to keep alive what God is trying to kill. Where your heart is where your treasures are (Matthew 6:21).

You have to plan on passing the test if you want to be promoted. Could it be the reason you haven't yet crossed over to the next level is that you keep failing the test... *the test of anger... the test of money... the test of loyalty... the test of love?* Could the reason you are still sick, broke and in trouble be simply because you keep going back fishing, when you should have gone forward?

Wrong reactions are deadly. Reactions are more powerful than your church attendance. When you are tested, and you will be, make sure you have the right kind of reaction. Think before you react. Have the God kind of reaction.

You were created to **Survive to Thrive!**

Surviving is when you solve your own problems.
Surviving to Thrive is when you solve the problems of others.

CONCLUSION

I am so honored that you have taken the time to read this book. It is such a privilege to sit down and to manuscript what God has laid on my heart in order to share it with you.

It is my goal to encourage you to start believing in yourself. I want you to know that God has put more in you than you have ever known. The real you is trying to surface. God is desperately trying to push you toward your future, while your past is trying to hold you back.

You are fearfully and wonderfully made (Psalm 139:14). You are not a mistake, an accident or a misfit. No, you are God's handiwork. What you are becoming will be the result of pressure. You need to know this. If you don't you will begin to doubt that you were destined to eat the grapes of blessing; believing that you deserve the grapes of wrath, which is certainly not true.

You are not just going to survive; you are going to thrive! You are going to rise above what should have and could have killed you. You future is not determined by where you came from.

Lamentations 3:25 tells us how good God is to those who wait for Him... Don't give up! Keep waiting; God is good to them who do.

KEYS TO WALKING IN A FAVORED LIFE!

1. *Build your own ship...* It will be custom to your fit.
2. *Create your own atmosphere...* It will determine your focus and your attitude.
3. *Be careful what you listen to...* It will decide what you believe.
4. *Qualify who you let around you...* Bad company can corrupt good morals.
5. *Be selective of whom you let mentor you...* They will decide what comes out of you.
6. *Re-prioritize your family to the top of your list...* They are God's gift to you.
7. *Learn to build a healthy "Self-Talk"...* This will decide what is replenished in you. "Self-Talk" builds expectation.
8. *Create a climate of peace.*
9. *Build a life of Faith through the Word of God.*
    a. Faith in God
    b. Faith in yourself
    c. Faith in others
10. *Cultivate a life of prayer.*
11. *Learn the law of adaptability. Dinosaurs are extinct because they couldn't adapt.*
12. *Remember that life is a gift, so do whatever you can to enjoy every moment.*
13. Create an attitude of thankfulness... Thankfulness replenishes the atmosphere for miracles to grow in.

MAY I INVITE YOU TO MAKE JESUS CHRIST LORD OF YOUR LIFE?

The Bible says, "That if you will confess with your mouth the Lord Jesus, and will believe in your heart that God raised Him from the dead, you will be saved. For with the heart man believes unto righteousness; and with the mouth confession is made for salvation." Romans 10:9, 10

PRAY THIS PRAYER WITH ME TODAY:

"Dear Jesus, I believe that You died for me, and that You rose again on the third day. I confess to You that I am a sinner. I need Your love and forgiveness. Come into my life, forgive my sins, and give me eternal life. I confess You now as my Lord and Savior. Thank You for my salvation! I walk in Your peace and joy from this day forward. Amen!"

Signed_____Date _____

Yes, I would like to be put on your mailing list. ☐

Name_____

Address_____

City_____State _____ Zip_____

Phone:_____Email:_____

FOGZONE MINISTRIES
P.O. Box 3707, Hickory N.C. 28603
1.888.328.6763 Fax: 828.325.4877
WWW.FOGZONE.NET

WHAT OTHERS ARE SAYING

Dr. Jerry Grillo lives what he teaches. It has been my privilege to be his personal friend for a number of years. He is a living example of a victorious leader. His church is a victorious church. If you can't succeed under this man of God you can't succeed anywhere. His revelation is life's fresh air in a stagnant world. He is one of the happiest and most exciting leaders I have known through my thirty-eight years of world evangelism. It is my privilege to recommend any book he has written.

Dr. Mike Murdock
The Wisdom Center

Dr. Jerry Grillo is truly a gift from God to my life. I love his passion, his purity and his painstaking commitment to purpose. It is very obvious that he loves the God he preaches to us about. Should you ever have the privilege of speaking into this life, you would know without a doubt he's one of God's favorites. Bishop Grillo, what a wonderful refreshing, what a wonderful friend!

Pastor Sheryl Brady
Sheryl Brady Ministries

Bishop Grillo is fast becoming a leading voice of authority... Having him minister at our Emotional Healing Conference became a valuable training session to our leadership and a needed breakthrough to many of our members. To say that Bishop Grillo is qualified to pen these pages would be an understatement. You hold in your hand a key to unlocking the life that God desires for you. I dare you to turn these pages with even the least little bit of expectation and watch as God begins to show out in your life!

Bishop Jeff Poole
New Hope International

TO INVITE DR. JERRY GRILLO TO SPEAK AT YOUR NEXT CHURCH CONFERENCE, BUSINESS MEETING OR TO SCHEDULE TELEVISION OR RADIO INTERVIEWS

WRITE TO:

FOGZONE MINISTRIES
P.O. BOX 3707
HICKORY, NC. 28603

OR EMAIL: FZM@FOGZONE.NET

FAX INVITATION TO 828-325-4877

OR CALL 1-888 FAVOR ME

[i] "Cunning." Cunning - Definition for English-Language Learners from Merriam-Webster's Learner's Dictionary. N.p., n.d. Web. 26 July 2017.

[ii] Nellibell49. THE OLD PROVERBIAL RECOVERY. N.p., 12 Mar. 2015. Web. 26 July 2017.

[iii] "About." IAV | About David Blankenhorn. N.p., n.d. Web. 24 July 2017.

[iv] Blankenhorn, David. "Fatherless America: Confronting Our Most Urgent Social Problem." Fatherless America: Confronting Our Most Urgent Social Problem, HarperPerennial, 1996.

[v] "H4196 - mizbeach - Strong's Hebrew Lexicon (KJV)." Blue Letter Bible. Web. 31 Jul, 2017. <https://www.blueletterbible.org//lang/lexicon/lexicon.cfm?Strongs=h4196&t=kjv>.

"H2076 - zabach - Strong's Hebrew Lexicon (KJV)." Blue Letter Bible. Web. 31 Jul, 2017. <https://www.blueletterbible.org//lang/lexicon/lexicon.cfm?Strongs=H2076&t=KJV>.

[vi] "Angel Abrea." AZQuotes.com. Wind and Fly LTD, 2017. 31 July 2017. http://www.azquotes.com/quote/542550

[vii] "Dale Carnegie." AZQuotes.com. Wind and Fly LTD, 2017. 31 July 2017. http://www.azquotes.com/quote/404137

[viii] The Man in the Arena - April 23, 1910 - Theodore Roosevelt Speeches- Roosevelt Almanac, 3 June 2012, www.theodore-roosevelt.com/trsorbonnespeech.html.

[ix] Murdock, MIke. "Why I Wrote This Book." 31 Reasons People Do Not Receive Their Financial Harvest, The Wisdom Center, 2007.

[x] "Definition of 'resource'." Resource Definition and Meaning | Collins English Dictionary. N.p., n.d. Web. 26 July 2017.

[xi] Provision Dictionary Definition | Provision Defined. N.p., n.d. Web. 26 July 2017.

[xii] "Thomas Jefferson Quotes." BrainyQuote. Xplore, n.d. Web. 24 July 2017.

[xiii] H5146 - Noach - Strong's Hebrew Lexicon (KJV)." Blue Letter Bible. Web. 26 Jul, 2017. <https://www.blueletterbible.org//lang/lexicon/lexicon.cfm?Strongs=H5146&t=KJV>.

[xiv] "G5281 - hypomonē - Strong's Greek Lexicon (KJV)." Blue Letter Bible. Web. 26 Jul, 2017.

<https://www.blueletterbible.org//lang/Lexicon/Lexicon.cfm?Strongs=G5281&t=KJV>.

[xv] https://www.megacatch.com/mosquito-faqs/mosquito-life-cycle.html

[xvi] Bielanko, Serge. "Pregnant for Years?! 20 Animals with Very Long Pregnancies." Babble. Babble, 13 Apr. 2017. Web. 31 July 2017.

[xvii] "barrier." YourDictionary, n.d. Web. 31 July 2017.
 <http://www.yourdictionary.com/barrier>

Read more at
http://www.yourdictionary.com/barrier#g6sBQorpJPshqkGI.99

WWW.DRJERRYGRILLO.COM

FOLLOW ME ON

 @BishopGrillo

 @BishopGrillo

 @BishopGrillo

 @Godstrongtv

RELEASING
THE F.O.G.
FAVOR OF GOD

▌Dr. Jerry A. Grillo, Jr.
Author, Pastor, and Motivational Speaker

Favor Conferences - Dr. Grillo is able to minister to many during seminars and conferences throughout America and around the world. Dr. Grillo's heart is to help encourage and strengthen Senior Pastors and leaders.

Books - Dr. Grillo has written over twenty -nine books including best sellers, "Saved But Damaged," "Pray for Rain." and many others.

Internet and Television - Dr. Grillo is anointed to impart the wisdom of God on Favor, Overflow and Emotional Healing. Online streaming and television has made it possible for Dr. Grillo to carry this message around the world into homes and lives that he would otherwise not be able to reach.

FINISHED WRITING?
YOUR PUBLISHING JOURNEY IS JUST BEGINNING

Let Us Publish Your Book

FOGzone Publishing is a helpful resource for first-time authors as well as experienced authors to offer services to best help with their book. Our goal is to make your vision a reality.

Being a published author is, ultimately, all about reaching out to your readers and knowing that you're able to share your story with them. But in order to make that successful crossover from writer to published author, you need to choose the publisher that best suits your publishing goals.

It is important to publish your book with an expert publisher that will work with you from start to finish. A reputable publisher should also have the necessary experience and expertise not only in book publishing, but also in book marketing, so your book can reach the widest audience possible.

Get Started today! Contact us @ fzm@fogzone.net or 828-325-4773

WWW.DRJERRYGRILLO.COM

FOGZONE
MEDIA & DESIGNS
FOGZONE PUBLISHING
WWW.FOGZONEDESIGNS.COM

Made in USA - Kendallville, IN
32333_9780997768930
12.15.2021 1727